Basic Geography & Weather Glossary

Basic Geography & Weather Glossary

HERON BOOKS

Published by
Heron Books, Inc.
20950 SW Rock Creek Road
Sheridan, OR 97378

heronbooks.com

Special thanks to all the teachers and students who
provided feedback instrumental to this edition.

Fourth Edition © 1995, 2023 Heron Books.
All Rights Reserved

ISBN: 978-0-89-739293-8

18 January 2023

At Heron Books, we think learning should be engaging and fun. It should be hands-on and allow students to move at their own pace.

To facilitate this we have created a learning guide that will help any student progress through this book, chapter by chapter, with confidence and interest.

Get learning guides at
heronbooks.com/learningguides.

For teacher resources,
such as a final exam, email
teacherresources@heronbooks.com.

We would love to hear from you!
Email us at *feedback@heronbooks.com.*

CONTENTS

Note: Words bolded in a definition are defined in the glossary.

A

Aborigines: the natives of Australia, who lived there long before any European settlers came.

air pressure: how much the air presses on the ground and other things. Air pressure helps weathermen predict the weather, because the pressure changes with different kinds of weather.

Alaska Range: a range of mountains in Alaska. There are several mountains in Alaska that are taller than any other mountains in North America.

alpine: "of the high mountains." Alpine plants grow low to the ground and are scattered around the mountains of the world. There may be a few short trees. Alpine plants have to be able to live with very cold temperatures, high winds and heavy snowfall.

Alps: a natural boundary mountain range that separates Italy from the rest of Europe.

altitude: how high above **sea level** the land is.

Amazon River: The biggest river in the world is the Amazon River in South America. This means that it carries more water than any other river.

Andes: the major mountains of South America. The Andes follow the Pacific coast of South America. They go all the way from the link to North America at Panama down to the southern tip of the continent in the region called Patagonia.

Antarctic Circle: a special **latitude line** drawn on maps at 66½ **degrees** south. Inside this circle there is at least one day every year when the sun does not set, and at least one day when it does not rise.

Antarctic Peninsula: a mountainous region of Antarctica that sticks far out into the ocean toward the tip of South America.

Appalachians: a major North America mountain range in the east. It separates the Atlantic coastal plains from the central lowlands of Ohio, Indiana and Illinois.

Arabian Desert: a desert that covers almost all of the Arabian Peninsula, which is just across the Red Sea from northern Africa. (There is another smaller desert called the "Arabian" or "Eastern Desert" between the Nile River and the Red Sea.)

Arctic Circle: a special **latitude line** drawn on maps at 66½ **degrees** north. Inside this circle there is at least one day every year when the sun does not set, and at least one day when it does not rise.

area: a small or large space of land on the surface of Earth.

Arkansas River: The Arkansas River has its source in the Rocky Mountains and flows east to the Mississippi River.

asteroid: The word asteroid means "like a star." Asteroids are big rocks. They revolve around the sun.

asteroid belt: There are lots of asteroids going in their own orbits around the sun in the space between Mars and Jupiter. This is called the asteroid belt because it is a bit like a belt. When you see asteroids with a telescope they look like stars, except they are moving.

atlas: a book of maps.

Atlas Mountains: these mountains separate the coastal regions of Algeria and Morocco from the Sahara Desert.

atmosphere: There is air around our planet. The blanket of air around Earth is called the atmosphere.

Australia: the continent between the Indian Ocean and the South Pacific.

autumn: the time of year when it starts to get cooler. Often the leaves turn pretty colors and fall off of the trees. Another name for autumn is **fall**.

axis: imaginary line on which Earth turns that goes down through the center of Earth.

B

barren: almost nothing grows there.

barrier: something that blocks the way. Oceans, mountains and rivers are barriers. They make it hard for people to get across.

basin: an area of land where water drains.

bay: a part of an ocean or lake that is partly surrounded by land. A bay is like a gulf, but it is usually much smaller.

biome: a type of **ecosystem** that covers large parts of Earth's surface. A biome might be big enough to cover a whole country or a big part of a continent.

blizzard: a big snowstorm with high winds.

borders: the lines on a map that divide countries and states.

boreal forest: the largest land biome in the world in Canada, Alaska, northern Europe, where the winters are long and very cold. It is called the boreal forest because the cold north wind, called the Boreas, often blows from the North Pole.

boundary: a line or thing that separates one place from another. The lines that separate counties, states, or countries are called boundaries. Often, a river or other **landform** may form part of a boundary.

Brazilian Highlands: major mountains in eastern South America.

breadbasket: a basket used for serving bread, but the word is used to mean a region where farmers grow a lot of wheat and other grains (because grain is made into bread).

Breadbasket of America: a **fertile plain** in the Midwestern U.S. where corn and wheat are grown.

breeze: when the air moves slowly.

brook: See **creek**.

C

calm: when the wind is not blowing at all, we say the air is calm.

canal: a waterway made by people. A canal is used for boats and ships to travel through land, and for getting water from lakes or rivers to other places that need it.

canyon: a narrow **valley** between mountains or hills, with a stream or river running along the bottom. A canyon doesn't usually have much flat space at the bottom.

cape: a point of land that juts out into water, usually wider than a **peninsula**.

capital city: the city where government leaders meet.

capitol: Government buildings are the buildings where people that run a state or a country work. The main government building is called the capitol (spelled with an "o").

cardinal: something that is the main thing.

cardinal direction: one of the four main **directions**. The cardinal directions are north, east, south and west.

Cascade Range: a mountain range that goes from Northern California through Oregon and Washington into Canada.

Caucasus Mountains: a range of mountains which, along with the Ural Mountains and the Caspian Sea, helps complete the natural **boundary** between Europe and Asia. They stretch from the Caspian Sea to the Black Sea north of Turkey.

Celsius scale (**C** for short): There are two different scales or sets of degrees often used to measure **temperature**. One is called the Celsius scale. It is named after the man who invented it.

Central America: all the countries between Mexico and South America.

Central Lowlands: an area of **fertile soil** towards the Appalachians.

Cero Aconcagua: the tallest peak in the Andes. It is 22,835 feet (6,960 meters) high, on the border between Chile and Argentina.

channel: a narrow body of water that connects two larger bodies of water.

chaparral: a smaller **biome** with small trees and bushes that stay green all year and have thick tough leaves. The weather is mild and it rains in winter, but summers are hot and dry like a desert.

city: a place usually much bigger than a town. There may be hundreds of thousand or even millions of people living in a city. A city is more important than a town because what happens in the city affects more people.

civilization: a group of people who have the same language, arts, sciences and rules to help them live together.

climate: what the **weather** of a region is like most of the time.

cloud: Although you can't see each water droplet in a cloud, you can see all the droplets together. That's what a cloud is—a lot of water droplets in the air. Some clouds are round and puffy like huge balls of cotton. Others are small and thin and look like feathers. Still others are thick and dark and come with storms. All clouds are the same in one way. They are all made of water.

cloudy weather: weather where there are clouds in the sky.

coast: a place where the land meets the sea, a seashore.

Coast Range: a range of mountains in North America close to the Pacific Ocean. In many places the Coast Range rises steeply right out of the ocean.

Coastal Plain: a major **fertile plain** in the eastern United States. It runs along the north coast of the Gulf of Mexico and along the shore of the Atlantic Ocean. It was these fertile lands that first attracted settlers from Europe.

coastline: the line of land that borders an ocean.

Colorado River: a major river west of the **Continental Divide**. Its source is high in the Rocky Mountains of Colorado. The Colorado River flows west and south through Utah and Arizona. There it goes through the Grand Canyon, and then on south along the western border of Arizona, until finally it reaches the western part of Mexico and empties into the Gulf of California.

Columbia River: the Columbia River forms the natural **boundary** between Washington and Oregon and empties into the Pacific Ocean.

comet: a comet is a ball in space. Comets are probably made of rock or ice and are not too big, maybe a mile or so across. Comets have a misty tail, like fog.

community: any group of plants and animals living together so that they affect each other.

compass: a small round instrument which has a needle that always points in the same **direction** when you hold it flat. The direction the compass points is called north.

compass rose: the face of a compass under the needle showing all the compass directions. It is called a compass rose because it looks something like the petals of a rose.

condensing: water changing from **water vapor** back into liquid, usually forming tiny droplets. This happens as the air holding the water vapor gets cooler.

Congo (or **Zaire**) **River:** a major river in Africa. It flows westward through the **rain forests** of central Africa, and empties into the Atlantic Ocean.

continent: on planet Earth, the largest land areas are called continents. Most of the people on Earth live on the continents.

continental climate: a **climate** away from the influence of the sea. It has a greater variation in temperature than a coastal climate at the same **latitude**—winters are much colder and summers much hotter. The largest areas in the U.S. with continental climates are in the Midwest and Northeast.

Continental Divide (also known as **Great Divide**): a **divide** at the top of the Rocky Mountains. The Continental Divide separates the waters that go to the Atlantic Ocean and the Gulf of Mexico from those that go into the Pacific Ocean.

continental United States: the part of the United States between Canada and Mexico. This means all the states except Alaska and Hawaii.

corals: little sea animals. Over time their skeletons build up into rock-like ridges along the sea bottom, called coral reefs. These reefs make homes for a great variety of colorful tropical fish.

country: an area of land on Earth where all the people feel they belong to the same group. An example of a country is the United States. There are many countries in the world.

county: the United States is divided up into states, and each state is divided up into government units called counties. A county is a smaller area in a state.

county seat: the town or city where the people who run the county work.

crater: big round holes on planets or moons. Some of these holes are made by asteroids crashing into the moon or planet. Other craters are made by volcanoes.

creek: a small stream. The water comes from rain or melting snow.

crescent moon: a crescent is a shape like a letter "C." The shape of the moon when you can only see a thin, curved part of it is called a crescent moon.

crossroads: a place where roads to different places cross each other. Sometimes the word crossroads is used for any place where travelers from many places meet. It is *like* a crossroads, even if it is not roads that cross. For instance Hawaii is sometimes called a crossroads, even though it is in the ocean and people get there by ships or airplanes instead of by roads.

cycle: when something goes around and ends up back where it started each time, like a wheel turning around and around.

cyclone: winds high up that form big swirling circles. Cyclones look something like the way water does when it goes swirling down a drain.

D

dam: something that slows or stops the flow of water in a river. Water collects behind the dam, forming a lake. Dams and lakes give a clue to the direction a river flows.

Danube River: a river in Eastern Europe that empties into the Black Sea.

day: 1. a day is the time it takes Earth to make one whole turn. We divide a day up into 24 hours. *Columbus sailed his ship for many days.*

2. day is the time when it is light outside. *I like to play during the day.*

Deccan Plateau: a major **fertile plain** in India.

deciduous: trees that drop their leaves are said to be *deciduous* (deciduous comes from a word that means "fall off").

degree: 1. a small step. A degree on a thermometer is a small step in temperature.

2. a way of dividing up circles. This is not the same as degrees used to measure temperature, but the same symbol is used (°).

delta: a triangle of flat land that forms at the **mouth** of a river. It is named after a triangle-shaped letter called "delta" in an old alphabet. The soil of a delta is usually very good for growing things during the times when the river is not flowing over it. The delta at the end of a large river can grow very large. For example, the delta of the Mississippi River in the U.S. is over 200 miles long.

Denali: See **Mount McKinley**.

desert: a place with very little water, so not much can grow there. A desert gets 0 to 10 inches of rain a year. A place that is so dry that very few plants and animals can live there.

dew: morning dampness on the ground. The dampness has settled out of the air onto the ground and onto other things as the air cooled off overnight. Often at night when the night air gets cool, **water vapor** in the air condenses into tiny droplets that settle on the grass. That is why grass is often wet early in the morning even when it isn't raining. This moisture on the grass is called dew.

direction: 1. the path along which something goes, points or lies. If you walk in the direction of a lake, you are going toward the lake.

2. the way something points or moves.

direction arrow: an arrow on a map that tells us which way north and other directions are on the map.

divide: a line at the top of a mountain range that is kind of like the peak of the roof of a house. It separates the waters that run down one side of the mountain range from those that run down the other side.

divided highway: a highway with a strip of land down the middle that separates the traffic going in different directions.

Don River: a river in Eastern Europe that runs south and empties into the Black Sea.

downpour: very heavy rain.

downstream: the direction in which a stream flows, toward its **mouth**.

downtown: the place in a city where most of the businesses are.

E

Earth: if we went way, way up and looked down, we would see something that looks like a huge ball. It has lots of water and big pieces of land. Sometimes there are clouds over the water and land. The name of this big round thing is Earth. Earth is made out of rocks and dirt and water and has air around it.

east: if you are facing north, east is the direction you point with your right hand if you point straight out to your side. East is always opposite west. East is always to the right when you are facing north and west is to the left.

Eastern Hemisphere: a name made up by people in Europe for the half of Earth that is mostly east from Europe. The Eastern Hemisphere includes Europe, Asia, Africa and Australia.

east-west lines: lines drawn on a globe that go around the globe in the east-west direction. These lines are used to locate places on a globe. The equator is a special east-west line.

economic geography: a part of **human geography** which has to do with how geography affects what kinds of things can be produced in a region.

ecosystem: landforms are a kind of "house" for the plants and animals that live there. All the living and non-living things that are there together are called an ecosystem (*eco-* means "house"). The living part of an ecosystem is the plants and animals and microscopic life. The non-living part includes things like sunlight, weather, water and soil.

Elbe River: a river in eastern Germany that empties into the North Sea.

ellipse: Earth travels around the sun in a slightly flattened circle. A flattened circle is called an ellipse.

environmental geography: has to do with how people affect and alter the natural landscape for their own purposes.

equator: an imaginary line between the Northern Hemisphere and the Southern Hemisphere. The equator divides the globe into two equal parts.

Equatorial Africa: the region of Africa around the Equator, where you can find **tropical rain forest** and **tropical grassland** with huge herds of animals.

Ethiopian highlands: The **highlands** of Ethiopia and Kenya average 4,000 to 10,000 feet (1,200-3,000 meters), but have higher peaks. The Ethiopian highlands have many peaks over 13,000 feet.

Euphrates River: a river in western Asia that flows through Iraq into the Persian Gulf.

Europe: a continent, bordered by the Atlantic Ocean on the west and the Ural Mountains to the east. To the south, the Mediterranean Sea separates Europe from Africa, but the southeast boundary is more complex. There the Black Sea, Caucasus Mountains and Caspian Sea form a **natural boundary** between Europe and Asia.

evaporate: liquid water changing to water vapor in the air. This happens as the water gets warmer, usually from the sun shining on it.

evening breeze: quite often land becomes cooler than water nearby after sundown. Then the air over the water starts to rise, and the air from the land blows toward the water to replace it. This is the evening breeze.

F

Fahrenheit (F for short): There are two different scales or sets of **degrees** on thermometers often used to measure **temperature**. One is called the Fahrenheit scale. It is named after the man who invented it.

fair weather: when the sky is clear and the weather is generally nice to be in, it is called fair weather.

fair weather clouds: puffy white clouds that will probably not rain.

fall: another name for **autumn**.

falling stars: falling stars are not really stars at all. They are small asteroids that are burning as they rush through Earth's air.

Far East: the lands of the Far East are China, Korea and Japan.

feature: something special about something that makes it look the way it does or be the way it is. For instance, one feature of a face is the nose in the middle.

Fertile Crescent: The flood **plains** of the Tigris and Euphrates Rivers are the eastern half of the Fertile Crescent, the coastal plains of the Eastern Mediterranean are the other half.

fertile plains: As rivers run from the mountains to the seas, they carry nutrient-rich bits of soil down into the valleys. Every time the rivers flood their **valleys**, they deposit tons of new soil nutrients. River valleys can be so wide that they eventually build up huge fertile plains that stretch for miles.

fertile soil: soil rich in plant nutrients.

flood: when there is lots of water where there usually is no, or less, water.

fog: when a cloud is near the ground it is a special type of **weather** called fog. Fog is made of tiny droplets of water. The difference between fog and clouds is just that fog is near the ground, and clouds are up in the air.

forest: land that is covered by trees. It takes at least 30 inches of rain a year to grow a forest.

freshwater: not salty like the oceans. Plants and animals that live in freshwater lakes and rivers are called freshwater life.

full moon: the moon when the part you can see is in the shape of a circle.

G

Ganges River: the river that carries waters from the **Himalayas** down into the Bay of Bengal. Every year the river floods land along the river downstream and deposits rich soil, making that area one of the most productive farming areas in all Asia. Because the area along the river can grow so much food, it also is one of the world's most highly populated areas. The waters of the Ganges are sacred to Hindus, who are followers of Hinduism, the major religion of India.

geography: the study of the surface of Earth. The word geography comes from a Greek word which means "writing about the earth." Geography includes not only the natural **features** of Earth's surface (such as mountains, rivers, climate and natural vegetation), but also how these physical features affect the lives of people, plants and animals.

glaciers: large masses of snow or ice. They form in places that are usually so cold that the glaciers can't melt away. Glaciers move very slowly down along **landforms** like mountains and plains. When they rub against landforms, they pick up lots of rocks and smooth off spots.

globe: a map of Earth that is round like a ball. A globe is a model of planet Earth. On a globe the oceans are usually colored blue and the land is a different color. A globe gives us an accurate idea of the shape, size and location of oceans and continents.

Gobi Desert: a desert in Mongolia. Although it is dry, it is more often cold than hot.

grassland: when there is some water, but not enough to grow a lot of trees, grass can grow very well. It takes 10 to 30 inches of rain a year to grow a grassland. Where the weather is not too extreme, grasslands are very good for growing wheat, corn and other grains.

gravity: our planet pulls everything on it toward the center or middle of the planet. This pulling of the planet is called gravity. Gravity holds things on the planet. Gravity pulls you toward the planet, and that direction is called down. The other direction is called up.

Great Basin: a region located between the Rocky Mountains and the Sierra Nevada Mountains where rivers and lakes have no outlet to the ocean. It extends from the Great Salt Lake in Utah south into southern California.

Great Basin Desert: a **desert** region that extends from the Great Salt Lake in Utah south into southern California.

Great Divide (also called the **Continental Divide**): a **divide** at the top of the Rocky Mountains. The Great Divide separates the waters that go to the Atlantic Ocean and the Gulf of Mexico from those that go into the Pacific.

Great Dividing Range: the major mountain chain in the continent of Australia. This mountain range runs along the eastern coast and separates it from the vast deserts of the interior. All of the biggest cities of Australia are located on the coast side of this range.

Great Lakes: between the United States and Canada there are five Great Lakes, and the waters of these lakes flow one into another. Lakes Superior and Michigan empty into Lake Huron.

Lake Huron empties into Lake Erie. Lake Erie empties, through the Niagara River and over Niagara Falls, into Lake Ontario.

Great Plains: a western area of fertile soil that includes North and South Dakota, Nebraska, Kansas and northern Texas.

Greenwich (GRIN-ij): there was a famous observatory for looking at the stars in England at a town called Greenwich. Early map makers decided to call the **longitude** line that went through Greenwich the zero **degree** longitude line.

grid: most maps have lines drawn on them that make squares. These lines are called a grid, which means a set of crossing lines. Grids help us find exactly where on a map things are.

Guiana Highlands: major mountains in northern South America. They are about 3,300 feet (1,000 meters) high.

gulf: part of an ocean or sea, like a **bay** but usually larger than a bay.

H

hail: rain that freezes into balls of ice on the way down. Hail comes down as balls of ice called hailstones. Hailstones are usually small, like raindrops, but if more water freezes onto these balls of ice, they can get as big as golf balls, or even as big as baseballs.

half moon: the moon when it is the shape of a half circle.

harbor: a small bay or other protected part of a body of water, used by ships as a safe place where they can drop anchor and "park."

hemisphere: half a ball (*hemi-* means half, and a sphere is a ball). When you are talking about Earth, a hemisphere means half of Earth.

highlands: a hilly or mountain region.

highlands of Ethiopia and Kenya: The highlands of Ethiopia and Kenya average 4,000 to 10,000 feet (1,200-3,000 meters), but have higher peaks. The **Ethiopian highlands** have many peaks over 13,000 feet and the **Kenya highlands** have one peak over 17,000 feet.

highway: a main road, big enough to handle a lot of traffic; a large street that connects cities and towns. Where it goes through the town the highway can look like another street. We use highways to go in a car from one city to another city.

hill: hills are like small **mountains**. They are not as high or as steep as mountains, and they are not as flat as **plains**. Usually they are more rounded on their tops than mountains.

Himalayas: the highest mountains in the world, in the southern part of Asia, north of India. Mount Everest, the tallest mountain in the world (29,028 feet or 8,848 meters high), is in the Himalayan Mountain range. The Himalayas form a **natural boundary** between India and the rest of Asia. The Himalayas are such a major natural boundary that India is often called a sub-continent, almost a continent of its own.

Huang River: See **Yellow River**.

Hudson River: a river in New York, one of the many small rivers east of the Appalachians which carry the waters of the **Coastal Plain** into the Atlantic.

human geography: the part of geography that focuses on what people do in relation to the physical geography, and why they do it.

Humboldt River: a river in Nevada where waters from the **Great Basin** collect. The Humboldt River ends in a place called the Humboldt Sink, a lake with no outlet that is sometimes dry.

hurricanes: large cyclones that get wound up very tight, and have very fast winds in them from high up right down to the ground. Hurricanes bring very big storms. A hurricane is miles across.

I

Indus River: a little to the east of the Persian Gulf in what is now Pakistan, the Indus River flows down from the Himalayan Mountains into the Arabian Sea.

inlet: a narrow strip of water reaching inland from a larger body of water such as a lake, bay or ocean.

international boundary: the boundary where two countries meet.

interstate highway: a big highway for travel in a state or between states. It is built for cars to go very fast.

island: a **landform** surrounded by a body of water such as an ocean, lake or river.

J

jet stream: sometimes on big weather maps you see pictures of high, fast winds that go zooming around Earth. These winds are called the jet stream. The winds in the jet stream go very fast, up to 125 miles an hour.

jungle: land covered very thickly with trees, vines and bushes. Real jungles are most often at the edges of **rain forests**.

K

Kalahari: a large desert on the west coast of southern Africa.

Kenya highlands: the **highlands** of Ethiopia and Kenya average 4,000 to 10,000 feet (1,200-3,000 meters), but have higher peaks. The Kenya highlands have one peak over 17,000 feet.

key: Often there are some little pictures or symbols on a map to tell you what is there. Sometimes it's hard to tell what those symbols mean. Usually there is a place on the map that tells what the symbols stand for. That is called the key for the map. Also see **legend.**

L

lake: a body of water on the land. Most lakes are freshwater, which means they are not salty like the oceans. A few lakes in the world are salty.

Lake Erie: the most southerly of the **Great Lakes**, Erie is fourth largest in surface area, but so much shallower than Ontario that it is the smallest in volume.

Lake Huron: Lake Huron is the second largest of the **Great Lakes**, but it has the world's largest fresh-water island.

Lake Michigan: Lake Michigan is the third largest of the **Great Lakes**, and the only one wholly within the borders of the United States; the others are shared with Canada.

Lake Ontario: the farthest east of the **Great Lakes**, Ontario is smallest in surface area, but it holds more water than Erie because it is much deeper.

Lake Superior: the biggest of the five **Great Lakes**. It is also the deepest, the farthest west and the farthest north.

landform: some of the big land **features** of Earth have shapes that are easy to tell and they are given specific names, like "mountain" or "hill" or "volcano." These special land features are called landforms.

Latin America: below the southern border of the United States, most of the people speak Spanish. In Brazil, most of the people speak Portuguese, which is a language very similar to Spanish. Both of these languages come from Latin, an old Mediterranean language. So all of these countries together are called **Latin America.** Latin America includes some countries in North America, all the countries in South America, and most of the islands in the Caribbean Sea.

latitude: distance measured on Earth's surface north and south of the **equator.** On a map or globe, lines of latitude are drawn running east and west, and you can use them to tell how far north or south you are.

latitude lines (lines of latitude): special curved lines are used to make a **grid** that can fit on a globe. The lines that go east and west are called lines of latitude. Latitude lines north of the equator are numbered north (N) latitude. The numbers go from 0° up to 90°. Latitude lines south of the equator are numbered south (S) latitude and the numbers also go from 0° to 90°. The equator is 0° for both north and south. The North Pole is 90° north and the South Pole is 90° south.

legend (also **key**): every map that has symbols on it needs a place on the map that tells what the symbols mean. This place is called the legend, or the key.

lightning: a crooked streak of very bright light that usually goes from the clouds to the ground or the ground to the clouds. Sometimes it just streaks between clouds. Lightning happens during violent storms. It is caused by electrical energy in the clouds.

Loire: a river in France south of Paris which empties into the Atlantic Ocean.

longitude: the distance that is measured on Earth's surface east and west of an imaginary line that passes through the town of **Greenwich**, England.

longitude lines (**lines of longitude**): special curved lines are used to make a grid that can fit on a globe. The lines that go north and south are called lines of longitude. Longitude is measured in **degrees**, but the lines do not stay the same distance apart like latitude lines. Instead they all cross each other at the poles. The longitude lines west of **Greenwich**, England, are numbered up to 180° W (west). The longitude lines east of Greenwich are numbered up to 180° E (east). The line for 180° E is the same as the line for 180° W.

M

mahogany: a kind of wood that comes from India and Southeast Asia.

Manchurian Plain: a major **fertile plain** in northeast China.

map: a drawing of how things would look if you were high above them looking down. Maps show where things are. Maps help us find things. A map is usually much smaller than the place it shows.

marine: comes from a word meaning ocean. Plants and animals that live by the sea or in the sea are called marine life.

marshes: lands that remain wet and soggy most of the time.

Mauna Kea: a tall peak in Hawaii, 13,796 feet (4,205 meters) high.

Mekong River: a major river of Southeast Asia. It flows south from China to form part of the border between Laos and Thailand. Then it goes through Cambodia and the southern tip of Vietnam into the South China Sea.

meridians: the lines of **longitude**.

meteor: another name for **falling stars**. Most meteors burn up before they touch Earth.

meteorite: a piece of stone or metal from a meteor that hit the ground.

Middle East: the part of Asia east of the Mediterranean Sea and north of the Red Sea that includes the Arabian Desert.

Mississippi River: the river in North America carrying the most water. The Mississippi comes down to St. Louis from Minnesota and goes on south to New Orleans. It forms **natural boundaries** for ten states before it empties into the Gulf of Mexico.

Missouri River: a major **tributary** to the Mississippi River. The Missouri River starts high in the eastern slope of the Rocky Mountains in western Montana. The longest river in North America is the combination of the Mississippi River and the Missouri River.

mist: rain so light and fine it is hard to tell if it is falling at all. It may be blown up or down by little gusts of wind.

Mohave Desert: a **desert** that extends from the eastern part of southern California down into Mexico.

Mongolia: a region north of China where there is a desert called the Gobi Desert.

Mongols: northern **nomads** who live by grazing their sheep and ponies on the thin **desert** grass, moving along when the grass is all eaten.

monsoon: steady winds in India and Southeast Asia that change direction just twice a year. In the winter they blow down from the north. In the summer they blow up from the south.

moon: 1. when we look in the sky at night we can sometimes see the moon. The moon is much smaller than the sun and even smaller than Earth. The moon *looks* about as large as the sun because it is much nearer to Earth than the sun is. The moon does not have water or air on it.

2. any natural large satellite moving around a planet.

morning breeze: in the morning when the sun comes up, the air over the water stays fairly cool, while the air over the land warms up from the sunshine and starts to rise. The cooler air over nearby water blows in to replace it. This wind is called a morning breeze because it only lasts until the air over the water gets mixed up with air from the land and isn't so much cooler any more.

mount (**Mt.** is short for mount): mountain or hill.

Mount Cook: a tall peak in New Zealand, 12,349 feet (3,764 meters) high.

Mount Elbert: in Colorado, it is the tallest mountain in the Rocky Mountains, 14,431 feet (4,399 meters) high.

Mount Everest: the tallest mountain in the world, 29,028 feet (8,848 meters) high. It is in the Himalayan Mountain range.

Mount Kosciusko: the tallest mountain in the Great Dividing Range in Australia. It is only 7,308 feet (2,228 meters) high.

Mount McKinley (also called **Denali**): the tallest mountain in North America, 20,320 feet (6,194 meters) high. It is in the Alaska Range.

Mount Mitchell: in North Carolina, is the tallest mountain in the Appalachians. It is only 6,684 feet (2,037 meters) high.

Mount Ranier: in Washington, is the tallest mountain in the Cascades. It is 14,410 feet (4,392 meters) high.

Mount Whitney: in Southern California, is the tallest mountain in the Sierra Nevada Mountains. It is 14,494 feet (4,418 meters) high.

mountain: parts of the land that rise high above the other parts of Earth's surface. Their sides are steep and they rise to a high top.

mountain chain: mountain ranges strung together in a row.

mountain range: a group of mountains.

mouth: the place where a river comes to an end at a large body of water such as an ocean is called the mouth of the river.

N

nation: another word for country.

national capital: the city where the leaders of the country meet and run the country.

national park: sometimes a country sets up a big piece of land to be a park for the whole country. These are called national parks. A very famous national park is called Yellowstone. It is in Wyoming.

natural boundary: a **boundary** that occurs naturally. It is not made by man. Natural boundaries separate land **features** and **ecosystems**. They can also separate water from land. Rivers, seashores and mountains are natural boundaries that are easy to see.

new moon: a new moon looks like no moon at all! New moon is what we call the moon when it is all dark. Sometimes we can see a faint line around the edge.

night: as Earth rotates, the sun shines on one side of it, giving light to that part. The area that does not get light is dark. It is night in that area. Night is when the sun is facing the other side of Earth and your side of Earth is in darkness.

Nile: the longest river in the world. It flows north through Egypt to the Mediterranean Sea.

Nile River Valley: part of the **Fertile Crescent**. The Nile River floods every year and keeps the **plains** along the river very fertile.

nomad: the people of the desert are called nomads or wanderers. They are nomads because they can stay at an oasis with their camels and a few goats only as long as the water lasts, then they have to move to another one.

noon: the middle of the day, when the sun is highest in the sky.

north: the direction a compass needle naturally points. The direction toward the **North Pole**.

North Africa: the part of Africa that includes the Sahara Desert.

North America: the northern part of the Western Hemisphere. It includes the United States, Canada and Mexico.

North American Desert: the name for the entire desert that is a large part of southwestern United States and Mexico. It is divided into several regions and each part is also called a desert.

North China Plain: a major fertile **plain** in China, in the **valleys** of the Yellow River and the Yangtze River.

North Pole: the farthest north place on Earth.

northeast: the direction between north and east.

Northeast: an area in the United States with many large cities. It includes Pennsylvania, New York, New Jersey, New Hampshire, Vermont, Maine, Rhode Island, Massachusetts and Connecticut.

Northern European Plain: a wide **fertile plain** that stretches across almost all of Europe north of the Alps from the Atlantic shore to the Ural Mountains.

Northern Hemisphere: when you are talking about Earth, a hemisphere means half of Earth. The northern half is called the Northern Hemisphere.

north-south lines: the lines drawn on a map that go from the North Pole to the South Pole.

northwest: the direction between north and west.

O

oasis: a place in the **desert** where water can be found and perhaps a few trees and a little grass.

Ob River: a river in Asia that flows north into the Arctic Ocean. It is frozen over most of the time.

ocean: Earth has big areas of water. These are called oceans.

ocean biome: the largest biome in the world since oceans cover three-fourths of Earth's surface. Ocean water is salty and animals and plants living in the ocean must be able to live in salt water. Plants and animals that live in the ocean usually are not able to live in water that is not salty.

Oder River: a river in western Poland that empties into the Baltic Sea.

Ohio River: a major river that is a **tributary** of the Mississippi. It comes from Pennsylvania and forms **natural boundaries** for five states before it reaches the Mississippi at the southern tip of Illinois.

orbit: the path Earth follows around the sun. The word orbit means "like a circle."

orient: the word orient means "east," and to orient yourself means literally to find out where east is, and face that way. When you orient a map, you turn the map so that east on the map aligns with east on the ground, and north on the map is north on the ground. This makes it easier to find the actual **direction** from where you are to places on the map.

outback: the interior of Australia is a huge, dry region of **desert** surrounded by **grasslands**, all of which is mostly wide open and flat. This interior land is called the outback, a name that Australians give to any part of Australia that is far away from town. To the west of the **Great Dividing Range** lies the main part of Australia and the huge flat interior of the continent known as the outback. It is used for grazing cattle and sheep, but it also has rich minerals in the ground. Settlements are widely scattered and the largest ones are mining towns.

overcast: when all of the sky is covered with **clouds**. You cannot see the sun when the weather is overcast.

P

Pacific Rim: the area around the edges of the Pacific Ocean where volcanoes have erupted and built up mountains.

Pampas: the largest **grassland** in South America. It is a huge, nearly treeless grassy **plain**, most of which is in Argentina. In South America most of the grasslands are used for raising cattle and sheep.

parallel: a line of **latitude** (because they run parallel to each other).

park: a piece of land for fun and play. It can be wild. It can be grassy or have flowers. It can have swings and playground equipment.

parkway: a wide road with grass, trees and bushes along its edges.

partly cloudy: weather where some of the sky is cloudy and some is clear.

peninsula: a **landform** almost surrounded by water. It is usually a long, fairly narrow piece of land connected at one end to a larger piece of land.

permafrost: ground that stays frozen all year round.

physical geography: the study of Earth's surface. In addition to mountains and rivers, it includes hills, plains, volcanoes, islands, and so on. But it also includes **climate** and the study of where different types of natural (wild) vegetation and animal life survive around the globe. The different **ecosystems**, such as forests, deserts, grasslands and tundra are all part of the study of physical geography.

plains: large areas of ground that are level or mostly level, with few trees.

planet: if we went way, way up and looked down, we would see something that looks like a huge ball. It has lots of water and big pieces of land. Sometimes there are clouds over the water and land. This big round thing is called Earth. A huge ball in space like this is called a planet. One of the nine very large balls that go around the sun.

plateau: a large flat piece of land that is higher than the land around it.

polar region (or **polar zone**): the region inside the Arctic Circle or the Antarctic Circle.

political geography: the setting of boundaries and the names of countries, states and regions are all part of political geography. Sometimes all of **human geography** is just called political geography, but that is not entirely correct, because there are other parts to human geography.

political map: a map that shows **boundaries**, such as between countries and states, and usually the most important cities. Political maps are part of **human geography** because the boundaries and names of the countries, states and regions are decided by people.

pond: a **landform** or **water feature** similar to a lake, but smaller.

predict: to tell what you think or know will happen in the future.

primary road: U.S. highways, interstate highways and state highways are the primary or main roads of an area.

Pyrenees: one of the major mountain ranges in Western Europe that form **natural boundaries**. The Pyrenees separate Spain from France.

R

rain clouds (storm clouds): dark gray clouds that will probably bring rain.

rain forest: the **forests** that get 6 to 30 feet of rain a year, and grow the biggest and thickest trees. Many, many different kinds of plants and animals live in these forests.

rain gauge: a container that is usually clear and marked on the side in inches so you can easily tell how much water is in it. But it can be any small can with a flat bottom and straight sides and an open top that will collect rain water.

rainstorm: a storm that brings rain.

raised relief map: a raised **relief map** is not flat. It is usually made of molded plastic and the height is shown by making the higher points higher than a flat surface. Usually it also shows difference in height the way a flat relief map does, with colors, lines, etc.

range: a group of mountains in a row.

reef: a ridge of rock or coral along the sea bottom that comes almost to the surface and can be dangerous to ships.

region: any large place or space on Earth.

relief map: a map that shows differences in height with different colors or special lines.

reservoir: often a city makes a lake by putting a dam on a river and takes its water from that lake. A lake made like this is called a reservoir.

revolving: moving in a circle. When we talk about Earth moving around the sun, we say it is revolving.

Rhine River: a river in West Germany that empties into the North Sea.

Rhone River: a river in France that empties into the Mediterranean Sea.

Ring of Fire: the **Pacific Rim** is sometimes called this because many of the volcanoes in that area are still active.

Rio Grande: a river that flows southeast from the Rocky Mountains to become the border between Texas and Mexico on its way to the Gulf of Mexico.

rise: we say the sun rises or comes up in the morning. It doesn't really rise or set, it just looks like that as Earth turns.

river: a large stream that takes water from higher land to lower land. A river may empty into a lake, an ocean or another river.

Rocky Mountains: the biggest mountain range in North America. The Rockies stretch from northern Canada and Alaska down through Texas and Mexico. They divide the high **plains** and low **deserts** to the west from the fertile **Great Plains** to the east.

rotate: to spin or turn around.

route: a way to go. It may be a road, or all the roads you take to get from one place to another.

S

Sahara Desert: probably the most famous desert in the world is the Sahara Desert in northern Africa. It is a hot desert of sand dunes with only an occasional oasis.

satellite: a smaller body or thing that goes around and around a larger body or thing. A satellite can be either a natural object, like our moon or Jupiter's moons or it can be a man-made object that goes around Earth.

savanna: grasslands near the **equator**. They are special because they stay warm or hot all year.

scale: 1. a way of telling how much smaller things in a map are than the real things. The scale compares the size of the drawing to the size of the real thing. Scales help to find distances on maps.

2. a set of **degrees** often used to measure **temperature**.

sea: the sea can be the whole wide-open ocean, or it can be an ocean, like the Atlantic Ocean, but it can also be a very large body of water that is partly enclosed by land. When sea is used this last way, the water might be salt water or it might not.

sea breeze: on the **seashore**, where there is a lot of cold water to keep the air cool, a gentle wind from the water to the land can keep going all day long. That wind is often called a sea breeze.

sea level: the usual or average level of the water at the seashore. The height of mountain tops and other land is measured as its distance above sea level.

seashore: the shore next to a sea.

season: one of the four parts of the year. The weather is usually different during each season. The seasons are spring, summer, fall and winter.

secondary road: roads smaller than highways.

Seine River: the river in France that flows through Paris to the English Channel.

set: we say the sun sets, or goes down, at night. It doesn't really rise or set, it just looks like that as Earth turns.

ship channel: a waterway for ships to travel in.

shore: a place where the land meets the water. The edge of a lake is called a lakeshore and a shore next to a sea is called the seashore or coast. It is a land **feature** but is not special or different enough to be a **landform**.

Sierra Nevada Mountains: a mountain range in Southern California between the Rocky Mountains and the Pacific Ocean.

sleet: rain that is so cold that some of it turns to ice as it falls.

Snake River: a river which starts in Yellowstone Park at Shoshone Lake, just west of the Continental Divide, flows westward though Idaho and Washington and joins the Columbia River, which carries the waters on to the Pacific Ocean.

snowflake: when the air is cold enough, the water in the air changes into ice. It freezes into tiny ice crystals that may grow to be quite big as they fall and more water freezes onto them. These crystals are called snowflakes.

snowstorm: a storm that brings snow.

society: a group of people who are alike in some way.

Sol: the name given to the sun by the Romans.

solar system: the group of planets going around the sun (Sol).

sound: 1. a long wide inlet of an ocean.

2. a broad channel between an island and a larger piece of land.

source: the beginning of a river or stream.

south: the direction opposite of **north**. In North America, it is the direction toward the South Pole.

South Pacific: the Pacific Ocean south of the **equator**.

South Pole: the farthest south point or place on Earth. The place where the **axis** comes out of Earth at the bottom.

southeast: the **direction** between south and east.

Southern Hemisphere: When you are talking about Earth, a hemisphere means half Earth. The southern half is called the Southern Hemisphere.

southwest: the **direction** between south and west.

sphere: another name for a ball.

spring: the **season** when it starts to warm up. The snow melts (if there is any) and flowers start blooming.

sprinkle: very light rain.

St. Lawrence River: the water from the **Great Lakes** that flows through Canada into the Atlantic Ocean. This river is big enough that ships from the Atlantic Ocean can use it to reach the Great Lakes.

star: a big, bright ball in space. Our sun is an example of a star. All other stars are so far away they look like little points of light.

state: a country, or part of a country. The United States has 50 different states in it.

state capital: The state capital is the *city* where government leaders meet.

state capitol: The "state capitol" (spelled with an "o") is different than a "state capital" (spelled with an "a"). The state capitol is *the building* where government leaders meet.

state highway: a road that goes through some cities in just one state.

storm: a strong wind, usually with heavy rain or snow. It is usually cold and cloudy and sometimes there is thunder and lightning. Storms usually last between one and three days.

storm clouds (rain clouds): dark gray clouds that will probably bring rain.

stormy weather: weather that comes with storms. It is usually made up of cloudy, windy and cold weather and always brings some form of rain.

strait: another word for **channel**. It often means a very narrow channel.

stream: the general word for flowing water, and the flow can be large or small.

summer: the **season** when the sun usually shines a lot and it is warmer.

sun: a huge, bright ball that we see in the sky during the day. People used to call the sun a planet but now we don't. The light from the sun shines on Earth and gives us light and heat. The sun is much bigger than Earth. It is very far away.

sunshine: the light and heat that comes from the sun. Sunshine is the most important thing that affects the **weather**. Sunshine warms the air and the ground.

swamp: lands that remain wet and soggy most of the time.

symbol: something that stands for something else. Symbols are used on maps to stand for things. Often, there isn't room on a map to draw things big enough so that you can see what they are, so symbols are used to show where things are. If you know what the symbols stand for, this makes the map roomier and clearer.

T

Taiga: the Russian name for the **boreal forest**.

teak: a kind of wood that comes from India and Southeast Asia.

temperate: not very hot and not very cold.

temperate forest: a forest **biome** where it is not too hot or cold, and which has four very distinct **seasons**. A great many plants and animals can live there.

temperate zones: the regions between the **tropics** and the **polar** regions. Most of the places where a lot of people live are in the temperate zones of the planet, especially in the North Temperate Zone.

temperature: how hot or cold something is. Something that is hot has a high temperature. Something that is cold has a low temperature.

thermometer: a tool used to measure how hot or cold the air is. *Thermo* means "temperature" and *meter* means "measure."

thunder: a rumbling sound that goes along with lightning. You always hear the thunder after you see the lightning flash because the sound takes longer to get to you than the light does.

Tigris River: a river in Asia that flows through Iraq into the Persian Gulf.

tornado: a whirling column of air shaped like a funnel. Tornados are usually 300 to 500 yards wide and do not last very long.

The winds in the center are strong enough to tear the roof off of houses and toss cars around.

town: a town has more people than a village and more stores and houses. There may be thousands of people living in a town.

Transantarctic Mountains: a major mountain chain in Antarctica. It divides the continent into two parts, East Antarctica and West Antarctica.

tributary: smaller streams that come together to make larger rivers or streams are called tributaries, because they *contribute* to the waters that make up the larger stream.

Tropic of Cancer, Tropic of Capricorn: at 23½ **degrees** of **latitude** north of the equator there is a special latitude line called the Tropic of Cancer. At 23½ degrees of latitude south of the equator is another special line, called the Tropic of Capricorn. These special latitude lines show how far north and south of the equator you can go and still have the sun be straight up in the sky sometime during the year.

tropical rain forest: the most important **rain forests**, which are the rain forests near the equator. It is believed that half of all the different kinds of plants and animals of Earth live in the tropical rain forests. They have far more kinds of plants and animals than any other place in the world.

tropics (tropic zone): the region between the Tropic of Cancer and the Tropic of Capricorn. You could say that the equator divides the tropics up into the northern tropic zone and the southern tropic zone. The tropics are warm or hot every day of the year, both day and night, and during the middle of the day the sun is always high overhead.

tundra: the huge area of flat land all around the North Pole, where there are no trees, and the ground is always frozen except for the upper two to three feet during the summer. The temperatures are low and the growing season is very short (about 60 days).

U

U.S. highway: a road that goes through some different states and keeps the same route number in each state.

U.S.A.: United States of America.

upstream: the direction toward the **source** of a river or stream.

Ural Mountains: a range of mountains on the dividing line from the Arctic Ocean almost down to the Caspian Sea. West of the Ural Mountains is Europe. East of the Ural Mountains is Asia.

V

valley: low land between mountains or hills. It usually has some land in the bottom that is more or less flat.

village: a small group of houses with a few stores and shops. There are often only one or two streets in a village. A village might have less than a hundred people, or at most a few hundred people.

Vistula River: a river in central Poland that empties into the Baltic Sea.

Volga River: a river in Eastern Europe that empties into the Caspian Sea.

W

water cycle: the journey of water through its different forms all around the world.

water vapor: tiny water particles in the air.

weather: how the air outside feels, how the sky looks, how much sunshine there is, and what is going on in the air is the weather. Weather is made up of sunshine, temperature, wind, clouds and rain. Weather can be called one of these four main types: fair, cloudy, foggy or stormy.

west: when you are facing north, west is to the left.

Western Hemisphere: a name made up by people in Europe for the half of Earth that is mostly west from Europe. It is the **hemisphere** that includes North and South America.

wetlands: lands that remain wet and soggy most of the time. Wetlands can be found in many places, but especially near rivers, lakes and oceans.

wind: wind is nothing more than moving air. You can make a small wind by blowing air out of your mouth. When the air outside is moving, the wind is part of the **weather**. When the air moves slowly, this is called a breeze. When the air is moving fast, it is called a wind. So wind has two meanings. It can mean "any moving air outside," or it can mean "fast moving air."

windstorm: when the winds of a storm are very strong, they can blow over trees and telephone poles and may even do damage to houses. This is called a windstorm if there is not much rain with it.

winter: the season when it is usually colder outside. In some places, it snows during winter. In other places, it rains more.

Y

Yangtze River: a major river in southern China, with its **mouth** at Shanghai.

year: we call the amount of time Earth takes to move once all the way around the sun a year.

Yellow River (or **Huang**): a major river in northern China, which has a very long history with the Chinese people, who started farming along its shores thousands of years ago.

Yellowstone Park: a **National Park** in the northwest corner of Wyoming.

Yellowstone River: a river which flows from Yellowstone Lake in Wyoming, just east of the **Continental Divide**, north through Montana into the Missouri River, which carries the waters on to the Mississippi River and the Gulf of Mexico.

Z

zero degree longitude: the early map makers decided to call the **longitude** line that goes through **Greenwich**, England, the zero degree longitude line. That was where they started counting the degrees from. It is labeled 0°.